Tending the Flock:

Shepherding Catholic Retirement Plans

Tending the Flock:

Shepherding Catholic Retirement Plans

Mary Brunson, AIF® & Judy Baba

Foreword by Mike Patterson, J.D., LL.M.

IFA Publishing
Irvine, California

FIRST EDITION

ISBN: 978-0-9768023-7-2

This book is dedicated to our families — on Earth and in Heaven. Sancta Maria, Mater Dei, ora pro nobis.

Acknowledgements

We would like to extend our sincere gratitude to the many people who have assisted in the creation of this book, especially Mark Hebner, Jackson Lin, Anne Page and Melissa Johnson.

We also thank the many individuals who have encouraged us in our mission to bring a prudent process for faith-based investing to Catholic organizations. A short list includes: Fr. Robert Spitzer, SJ, Fr. Seamus Finn, OMI, Harry Markowitz, Bruce Egnew, Tim Busch, Berni and Rob Neal, Mike Patterson, John Peiffer, Rod Crane, Kahne Krause, Kurt Ritter, Tim Psomas and Bruce Corcoran.

And finally, to the Holy Spirit for breathing into us strength, courage, fortitude, and inspiration.

Table of Contents

Foreword

Until now, retirement plan sponsors within Catholic organizations have been left without a resource to advise them of the best practices they should be implementing to ensure their workers have a secure retirement. These servants, who have dedicated their life to the Church, deserve to receive world-class retirement benefits.

Tending the Flock: Shepherding Catholic Retirement Plans is a well written, comprehensive, practical guide for plan stewards of Catholic organizations. This book provides an invaluable resource for building a new secure retirement plan structure in today's post-Great Recession economy and is a must read for anyone involved in retirement plans within the Church.

As counsel for numerous Catholic organizations around the country, I have been counsel in numerous fiduciary obligation lawsuits and have seen the negative impact litigation has on everyone involved. It is my considered opinion that if the guidelines set forth in this book are followed, fiduciary obligation litigation will be reduced substantially. I believe this book should be required reading for all Archbishops, Bishops, Chief Financial Officers, and plan sponsors of Catholic organizations.

The genius to this book is that it not only lays out the duties and responsibilities of fiduciaries, but it does so in a way that is consistent with the Church's mission and core values.

About Mike

Mike Patterson, J.D., LL.M.

Mike Patterson, J.D. LL.M. is the Senior Principal and President at Patterson Buchanan. He is a nationally recognized trial attorney, having tried more than 100 cases to verdict in both federal and state courts, and has served as an expert witness on fiduciary duty in numerous matters throughout the country. Mr. Patterson concentrates his practice on high profile litigation and ERISA cases. He has represented various archdioceses throughout the country; scores of school districts; numerous cities, counties, and fire districts; and many well-known private clients in litigation. He has handled class action lawsuits on fiduciary duty issues involving thousands of participants throughout the country. Representative jury trial cases include:

- Fualaau v. Highline School District
- Johnson v. Catholic Community Services
- Biteman v. Archdiocese of Seattle
- Howard v. Catholic Community Services
- Jones v. Port Angeles School District
- J.D. v. Bellingham School District
- Davis v. Tacoma School District
- Kintle v. Catholic Community Services

He holds a Bachelor's degree from Gonzaga University, a Juris Doctorate from Notre Dame, and a Master's of Law from New York University.

He is an invited member of the Notre Dame Lawyer (Law Review), and holds numerous board positions for the Archdiocese of Western Washington, Gonzaga University, Legatus International and various Catholic apostolates.

Accolades

In this age of hidden and unexpected liabilities a fiduciary and Churchmen must consider how they can protect the assets of the Church and the People of God thru assigning liability to a third party--this short read explains just how. The authors also detail how to apply an investing approach that is prudent and socially responsible--an almost impossible task thru open market investments. I am sure you will enjoy the text of this manual of how to approach investment of Church retirement funds in a socially responsible and prudent manner.

Timothy R. Busch, J.D., C.P.A.
Founder of The Busch Firm, co-founder of Magis Institute

As Bishops, priests, religious, and laymen offer their lives to the Church, they deserve our care both during and after their faithful service. The authors have provided a clear turn by turn roadmap to understanding and implementing benefit plans that reveal a straight forward path to honoring those in a way commensurate with their self-giving to us.

Dan Burke
Executive Director of EWTN's National Catholic Register
and Founder of the Avila Institute for Spiritual Formation

The authors provide a clear and understandable process for the design and implementation of a Catholic faith based defined contribution plan. The book is well written and is a must read for all Diocesan CFO's whose organizations provide or are contemplating a defined contribution plan. The authors provide an insightful and logical approach for investment vehicle selection with easy to understand investment terminology. A major strength of the book is that the authors provide possible document language to incorporate into the plan documents. The final chapter is a powerful summary of how to construct a secure and well-run church retirement plan.

LOREN SCHILLINGER
Finance Officer, Diocese of Cheyenne, WY

I started reading this book, and had to finish it in one go. It outlines everything those involved in retirement plans need to know, and points out those things we probably never thought about. Everyone thinking of changing their plan needs to read this. I feel privileged, being one of the first persons able to read this book, and provide my comments on it. It is extremely well written, understandable for those with limited knowledge of retirement plans. I will use this book for my understanding about our retirement plans, and for distribution amongst my committee members.

AAD DE LANGE
CFO, Catholic Diocese of Jackson, MS

About Mary

Mary Brunson, AIF®

Mary Brunson is the Vice President of Investing for Catholics, a division of Index Fund Advisors, Inc. She embarked on the specific mission of Investing for Catholics to advance education about faith-based, prudent investing with a strategy that seeks to enhance both spiritual and financial returns. This effort is designed to facilitate a deepening of faith and stewardship by providing a sound investment approach to Catholic organizations. Mary provides fiduciary advice and services to religious orders, Archdioceses and dioceses, endowments and foundations, as well as individuals. Mary is a board member for the Magis Center of Reason and Faith, an institute spearheaded by Father Robert J. Spitzer, S.J. She is also the current National Chair of the Spirituality Commission for the National Council of Catholic Women (NCCW), the women's organization representing the United States Conference of Catholic Bishops, and she is a frequent writer for the organization's publication. Mary earned a Bachelor of Arts degree from University of California, Irvine. Her professional designations include a Series 65 license, and she is an Accredited Investment Fiduciary (AIF). She is married and has four children.

About Judy

Judy Baba

Judy Baba is the liaison for Institutional and 401(k) Retirement Services at Index Fund Advisors (IFA). In this role, she provides assistance to retirement plan participants, helping them understand the various aspects of the retirement plan process. She also supports IFA advisors as a Client Services Representative in setting up individual and corporate brokerage accounts. In previous positions, Judy has worked with individuals and organizations both in the development of new retirement plans and administration of legacy plans by helping participants understand their benefits and working with plan sponsors to apply prudent processes to plan management. Judy received a Bachelor's degree in Journalism from the University of Southern California, where her writing career was launched. She has since been involved with many communications and writing ventures. She is married with two grown daughters and lives in Irvine with her husband Duane.

Chapter 1

Our Purpose

"Human work proceeds directly from persons created in the image of God and called to prolong the work of creation by subduing the earth, both with and for another."

—The Catechism of the Catholic Church

The value and importance of human labor is a well-wrought subject within Catholic teachings throughout the centuries. The Catechism further tells us, "Work honors the Creator's gifts and talents received from Him."

Those who have worked for the Church, its global missions and ministries, have woven themselves into a centuries-old tapestry that continues to reveal the beauty, mercy and glory of God. And through their toil, corporal works permit the glorification of God, the sanctification of the giver, and the evangelization of the recipient. It is a magnificent story—one that continues to unfold each day.

The Catholic Church has moved mountains through global ministries over the centuries. Her imprimatur on healthcare and education is undeniable, as billions have benefitted from the storied institutions built from impassioned ministries—and they continue as we speak.

Well-honed standards and practices have led to advances for the elite and the poor alike.

It is a proud history for the Church—made possible through the collaborative effort of the faithful who have placed their call to serve the Church at the forefront of their work. It is for them we write this book.

The time has come for us to prioritize helping those who serve the Church. What you give to others through your ministries, you also need to give to yourself and your employees. This book is a practical guide to the global precepts and best practices Catholic organizations can implement to administer an effective and efficient retirement plan that will help ensure that your workers have sufficient income to and through retirement.

Best Practices Lead to A Better Outcome

You may currently have in operation one or more retirement plans that more or less do the job, but have their own inherent complexities that may not be in keeping with up-to-date best practices. "If you have seen one church plan," observes Rod Crane of TIAA-CREF, "you have seen one church plan." As Director of Institutional Client Relations, Public Sector Market at TIAA-CREF, Rod has seen hundreds of plans, and each one is unique.

It is challenging to operate ad hoc plans. Chances are that the details involved feel overwhelming, and when this happens, a common human response is to procrastinate even when you know you need to take action. Inaction leads to not being able to "see" the end goal

– which is to provide a secure retirement for your workers—who commit to the Church and its ministries.

It is important to know that there is a clear way to mold these disparate pieces into a plan with a purpose – a plan that operates in the best interests of participants, not only because they deserve it, but also because the plans themselves require that they be operated this way. Not only do you want to do this, you need to do this.

The solution is not without work, but it's much easier than what you are probably doing right now, which is likely akin to banging your head against the wall.

It's really that simple.

Chapter 2

OUR ROLE

As a member of your organization's retirement plan committee, you play a critical role in overseeing the plans that are part of the traditional Catholic mission of assisting employees in preparing for retirement. This stewardship role has become even more critical and challenging in these difficult economic times.

It is no secret that the defined benefit retirement plans that many Catholic organizations have traditionally relied upon have grown more costly and onerous at the same time organizations are stretching hard to fund all of their missions – and many existing defined contribution plans are cumbersome to manage and difficult to understand.

It is clear that something needs to change.

So where do we start — with trying to narrow down the seemingly dizzying array of plan and investment options that we are offered before we take the time to establish the goals and objectives of the overall plan?

In our work, we have found that starting with a discussion of plan options is like trying to install doors and windows into a house before the foundation is set and the walls have been framed. The best place to start is with the fundamental question: "Why we are here?" Another foundational element is the committee's understanding of the fiduciary mantle they have taken up as plan stewards.

As described by fi360, a leading fiduciary training and resources organization in the U.S., stewards stand at the top of the fiduciary pecking order. They are generally named as fiduciaries in trust or pension plan documents and essentially hold all fiduciary responsibilities unless they formally take steps to delegate some of those responsibilities to other prudent experts, such as advisors or managers.

What is a Fiduciary?

A fiduciary duty is a legal duty to act solely in another party's interests. Parties owing this duty are called fiduciaries. The individuals to whom they owe a duty are called principals. Fiduciaries may not profit from their relationship with their principals unless they have the principals' express informed consent. They also have a duty to avoid any conflicts of interest between themselves and their principals or between their principals and the fiduciaries' other clients. A fiduciary duty is the strictest duty of care recognized by the U.S. legal system. Examples of fiduciary relationships include those between a 3(38) Investment Managers for ERISA[1] 401k Plans, Registered Investment Advisors and their clients, lawyers and their client, guardians and their wards, and directors and their shareholders.

[1] Please see the definition of ERISA in the Glossary.

ERISA defines a fiduciary as anyone who exercises discretionary authority or control over a plan's management or assets, including anyone who provides investment advice to the plan. Of course, Catholic organizations are formally exempt from complying with ERISA when electing Church plan status – but this does not equate to a lack of fiduciary duties. There are many benefits to defining your committee's fiduciary role and aligning your organization's retirement plans according to regulations outlined by ERISA:

- The levels of "care, skill, prudence, and diligence" required by ERISA already largely apply to non-ERISA plans. Many of the state laws regulating plans either mimic ERISA provisions, reference them directly, or draw heavily upon them.

- Learning the best practices and processes that come from the deep and rich experience of ERISA plans will lead to a strong foundation upon which successful retirement plans can be built, thus allowing organizations to move forward in a positive and successful way.

- Rod Crane, Senior Director of TIAA-CREF's Government and Religious Markets, explains the reason for adopting ERISA standards this way: "The worst risk from any perspective is a failed plan – a failed plan that doesn't get participants to an adequate secure retirement, a plan that does not meet the mission objectives of the church, a plan that does not meet the employer objectives of the church as an employer for attracting and retaining and having the timely retirement of older workers from the work force. Failed plans are much worse than taking on a little bit of manageable fiduciary risk." [2]

[2] Rod Crane's complete comments can be viewed at http://investingforcatholics.com/films/rod-crane-tiaa-cref.aspx

- ERISA standards provide a cornerstone for successfully accomplishing your greater mission — the secure retirement of your employees.

As you probably know, or may have astutely guessed, all of the above are the overarching duties for fiduciaries outlined by ERISA:

WHICH OF THE FOLLOWING IS A MAIN RESPONSIBILITY OF A FIDUCIARY UNDER ERISA?

- ☐ Act with Loyalty
- ☐ Act Prudently
- ☐ Diversify Plan Assets
- ☐ Act in Accordance with the Plan's Terms
- ☐ Pay Only Reasonable Plan Expenses
- ☐ All of the above

Act with Loyalty – Fiduciaries must put any personal or private interests aside and always act in the best interests of the plan participants and beneficiaries.

- Self-dealing, conflicts of interest, and even the appearance of impropriety must be avoided at all costs. Self-dealing occurs when a fiduciary stands to personally gain financially from a decision.

- A fiduciary is obligated to avoid conflicts of interest whenever possible and to manage or mitigate and disclose unavoidable conflicts in such a way that the employees' best interests are served.

Act Prudently – Fiduciaries must use the same degree of "care, skill, prudence and diligence, under the circumstances then prevailing that a prudent man acting in a like capacity and familiar with such matters would use in the conduct of an enterprise of a like character and with like aims."

- The most common state prudence laws applying to non-ERISA plans today are identical to ERISA's "prudent investor" standard. Other prevailing laws apply a "prudent person" standard. They all point to the same goal: fiduciaries must behave as if their own money is on the line.

- Prudence focuses on the **process** for making fiduciary decisions, i.e., on the manner in which plans and investments are managed rather than the outcomes achieved. Elements of a prudent decision making process include:
    - Identifying and analyzing relevant information
    - Using experts where necessary
    - Retaining information received
    - Documenting decisions and processes

Diversify Plan Assets – Fiduciaries must select appropriate investment options that are consistent with the unique needs of their organization.

- ERISA requires that fiduciaries diversify plan' investments to minimize risk of investment loss. When choosing investments, fiduciaries should select investments with different objectives and risk/return characteristics. For participant-directed plans, a broad range of investments should be offered so participants are able to build portfolios that are appropriate given their goals and risk tolerances.

- Where a plan sponsor lacks investment expertise to select investment options, it is advisable to hire someone with that professional knowledge to carry out the investment and other functions.

Act in Accordance with the Plan's Terms – Each plan has certain key elements, including a plan document that describes the benefit structure and guides day-to-day operations.

- It is important that you become familiar with the plan document, particularly if it is drawn up by a third-party service provider, and to periodically review the document as well as the plan's administrative procedures to make sure they remain current.

Pay Only Reasonable Plan Expenses – When deciding on service providers and plan investments, fiduciaries will want to understand the fees and expenses charged and the services provided.

- While the law does not specify a permissible level of fees, it does require that fees charged to a plan be "reasonable."

- After careful evaluation during the initial selection, fees and expenses should be regularly monitored to determine whether they continue to be reasonable and plan participants are not paying more than they should.

Embracing and implementing the fiduciary practices specified by ERISA is the first step toward organizing your approach for the stewardship of your organization's retirement plans. As a result, the plans and investments under your care will be managed in a more disciplined and defensible manner. This is because the fiduciary standard of care is a ***process*** standard and ERISA brings a process that leads to better outcomes. As fi360 puts it, "*It is also likely your work* *will be perceived by others as more valuable because sound processes consistently applied are easier to explain, understand and be recognized as trustworthy."*

Helpful Resources

There are many resources on the internet which can be consulted to expand your understanding of the fiduciary process. A great place to start is with the Department of Labor publication "Meeting Your Fiduciary Responsibilities" at www.dol.gov/ebsa/publications/fiduciaryresponsibility.html.

Also helpful is the fi360 handbook "Prudent Practices for Investment Stewards," which can be found on the web at: www.fi360.com/main/pdf/handbook_steward.pdf. While the fi360 handbook is quite detailed and technical, it breaks the fiduciary process down into a series of practices that follow a simple four-step "fiduciary quality management system": Organize, Formalize, Implement and Monitor.

The first step, Organize, is initiated with understanding what it means to be a fiduciary and then adopting ERISA standards as the cornerstone of your prudent processes. In the next chapter, we will examine a set of best practices for the committee itself that will strengthen this cornerstone and serve as the basis for the steps to follow.

Chapter 3

Our Job

In service to the mission of the Church to protect the human dignity of employees by helping ensure their income to and through retirement, the tasks at hand for the committee mirror the responsibilities of any general manager, which are to:

- *Identify goals and objectives of the plan*
- *Determine how resources will be allocated*
- *Formalize a written plan*
- *Implement the written plan, and on an ongoing basis,*
- *Monitor results to ensure that the goals and objectives of the written plan are being met*

One key difference between the retirement plan committee and a general manager, however, is that the committee is a group made up of disparate individuals with diverse strengths and opinions who are charged with coming together to make collaborative decisions that are deemed to be in the best interests of the plan's participants. Research has shown that, working together, groups tend to make better decisions than most individuals, particularly when facing complexities such as those that face retirement plan committees.

Working Together Works

Empirical evidence shows that committees work best when everyone participates fully. In fact, the ability of a committee to make superior decisions depends upon how well it functions as a team with a common objective while embracing its diversity of perspectives. This concept has been demonstrated by Scott E. Page, Professor of Complex Systems, Political Science, and Economics at the University of Michigan, who introduced the Diversity Prediction Theorem. His model shows that the collective ability of a group is made up of both the individual abilities of the group's members and the diversity of their thinking.

Further, if a group of problem solvers all agree on an objective, then having diverse ideas about how to achieve the objective leads to better decision making. Because your committee has the advantage of having and understanding a common objective - to provide a retirement plan that operates in the best interests of your participants – we can focus on how best to capitalize on the diversity of ideas.

Pitfalls to Avoid

Just as research suggests that groups tend to outperform individuals on the types of responsibilities faced by retirement plan committees, it is also true that groups can be derailed by behavioral hurdles – hurdles that can quash the free flow of diverse ideas. Some key behaviors that can lead to pitfalls include:

> **Groupthink** – the phenomenon that occurs when the desire for group consensus overrides people's common sense desire to present alternatives, critique a position, or express an unpopular opinion.

The desire for group cohesion effectively drives out good decision making and problem solving. According to Rick Gay, Purchasing Manager for the Baltimore Unified School District, the term "Groupthink" was coined by Irving Janis in 1972 who researched why a team reaches an excellent decision one time and a disastrous one the next. He found was that a "lack of conflict or opposing viewpoints led to poor decisions, because alternatives were not fully analyzed, and because groups did not gather enough information to make an informed decision," Gay cited. Janis began exploring the concept of Groupthink by analyzing the events that led to the failed Bay of Pigs invasion of 1961, where U.S. soldiers attempted to overthrow Castro's Cuban government.

The polarizing effect of groups – the tendency of groups to make more extreme decisions than individuals do acting on their own, according to a Vanguard study called "Group Decision-Making: Implications for Investment Committees." The study concluded that the direction a group's thinking takes depends on the group's initial views. For instance, groups with initially cautious views will at times make a more cautious decision than members would have made individually. Similarly, groups with initially risky views may make a riskier decision than the individuals would have made acting alone. In any group trying to make a decision there is likely to be an initial preference in one particular direction. Those who don't initially agree with that decision are likely to change their mind to agree with the majority.

Overconfidence – the human tendency to report flattering beliefs about oneself and believe that one is above average, sometimes referred to as the Lake Wobegon effect (named after

Garrison Keillor's fictional town where "all the children are above average"). The afore-mentioned Vanguard study also found that groups who are overconfident can engage in perfunctory and superficial discussions that can also lead to two debilitating biases: confirmation bias and shared-information bias. Both tendencies can lead to ineffective decision making.

- ***Confirmation bias*** *is a group's tendency to seek out information that confirms its initial views. We as humans tend to look for data that confirms our view of the world.*

- ***Shared information bias*** *occurs when groups only discuss information that is available to all group members—so they do not leverage the group's full investigative resources.*

The committee can avoid these pitfalls by:

- Viewing disagreement as a necessary, helpful characteristic of great teams

- Fostering open discussion, encouraging members to freely contribute their thoughts, ideas, and opinions

- Keeping an open mind and avoiding criticism

- Inviting input and information from trusted partners

Adopt a Charter

Achieving robust decision making and smoothing the functioning of their team is the basis of one of the best practices adopted by committees that are among the most successful – and that is creating and adopting a charter. One reason for this is that in reframing the committee's thought processes to recharacterize disagreement as necessary for healthy discussions, members will also want to be cautious of gridlock or compromises that can weaken their decisions.

It helps smooth the process when the committee establishes a few ground rules in their charter for resolving disagreements and achieving resolution. This will allow the committee to focus on the issues that require thought and insight rather than taking time to negotiate otherwise straightforward decisions.

The basic outline of the charter will include the committee's mission statement and a general section about housekeeping items, such as how often meetings will be held. Then the charter should focus on:

- The committee's role as a fiduciary
- The approach the committee will take in decision making
- The roles and responsibilities of each individual in the functioning of the committee and the recognition that every member has a role

Next Steps

With the cornerstone of understanding fiduciary practices and of basing decisions on a diversity of well-explored ideas firmly in place, the committee is now in a position to look at where we are and where we want to go as we take the next step to formalize the process for getting there.

Chapter 4

Our Path

Journalist Chuck Palahniuk has observed that "If you don't know what you want, you end up with a lot you don't." Without proper goal-setting, achieving objectives is a hit or miss proposition—at best. This is why the priority for the retirement plan committee is to define goals based on fulfilling your primary duty and objective of providing a program that will give your participants a path for plan success and retirement readiness.

Formalizing these goals will create a roadmap to keep the retirement program on course. And as with any good directions, the place to start this road map is with Point A.

Start with Point A

Identifying Point A starts with two questions: Who are our participants, and what is or is not working with the current program?

In answer to the first question, if your participants are like most Americans, their confidence in their ability to retire comfortably remains at a historically low level, according to the Employee Benefit Research Institute (EBRI) 2013 Retirement Confidence Survey. [1]

The study shows that workers are preoccupied with increased cost of living expenses and debt. Their savings rates have declined regardless of their awareness of the need to save for retirement. And a majority does not have a clear idea of how to set savings goals. There is a bright spot, however — 82% of those who are eligible for their employer-sponsored retirement plan use it to save for retirement.

Knowing that participants depend upon their employer-sponsored plan to prepare for retirement will help the committee put into context the need to understand and wrap its arms around the answers to the second question: What is working and what is not working with the current retirement program?

This understanding starts with a review of the current plan(s), and there is no better place to start than with the filing system. This may seem surprising, but the importance of well-structured documentation cannot be overstated. It is an integral part of the fiduciary processes that plan sponsors implement to ensure the success of retirement plans.

In most cases, there will be existing audit files in both paper and electronic formats. This is a good time to ask staff if the current document management systems are consistent and well organized. Can all existing plan documents be found easily – including any signed agreements and amendments as well as any adoption agreements, summary plan descriptions and/or an Investment Policy Statement? Is all ongoing reporting routinely stored? Is there a retrieval system for the documented decisions and meeting minutes of the investment committee?

---

[1] The Employee Benefit Research Institute is a private, nonpartisan, nonprofit research institute based in Washington, DC, that focuses on health, savings, retirement, and economic security issues. For more information go to www.ebri.org or www.asec.org

Once assured that the audit files are in good order (a goal in and of itself!), the committee can examine the plan documents and become familiar with the existing program, its features, and its costs to participants – and determine what is or is not working for the participants as well as for the organization. Just as participants face the realities of tough economic times, so too do organizations. Plan sponsors must make difficult choices. The bright spot is that these difficulties make this a good time for the retirement plan committee to step back and take a hard, critical look at their program in an effort to manage risks better for the organization while making the plan work as well as possible for the participants.

POINT B: THE ROAD MAP

Once the committee has identified the salient parts of Point A – who are our participants, and what is and is not working with our current program – the next task is to determine Point B and the goals and objectives for getting there. Identifying Point B starts with this important question:

- How do we deliver a retirement program that serves the needs of our participants for a secure retirement while managing risks for the organization?

Most committees are immediately familiar with the documentation needed to create an Investment Policy Statement (IPS). The IPS typically outlines the investment roles and responsibilities of the plan, permissible asset classes, and information on other matters such as fee analysis criteria, diversification guidelines and benchmarks. What the

IPS does not describe, however, is how plan participants will obtain an adequate benefit or even what the benefit should be.

Laying out a foundation for this type of information is becoming more important as organizations make changes in their retirement programs that require participants to assume a greater share of the risk and responsibility for their own retirement income. If we look at most 401(k) plans in the corporate world, we see that they do not define a retirement income target – so is it any wonder that their participants also fail to understand how to analyze and set retirement savings goals for themselves?

Recognizing this gap in understanding, retirement plan committees are embracing the concept of "plan design with a purpose," which is expressly intended to better guide participants to positive outcomes. With this type of design in mind, we recommend the adoption of a Benefits Policy Statement (BPS).

A good starting place for creating a BPS is with a template document, such as the one provided by TIAA-CREF. As indicated on TIAA-CREF's template, the BPS will "set the framework under which the retirement benefit program and its component plans are to be designed. All other program policies are either informed by or based on the Benefits Policy Statement." Rod Crane, Senior Director of TIAA-CREF's Government and Religious Markets, likes to point out that, as Yogi Berra once said, "If you don't know where you are going, you will wind up somewhere else."[2] The BPS is the foundational piece that provides a road map of where the retirement program is going.

More specifically, Crane explains that the BPS should answer the primary question, "Is this plan's primary purpose to provide retirement income for life or as a wealth accumulation vehicle? Asking and answering that question separates you very clearly from what the standard answer has been for the corporate 401(k) world, which is that this is a wealth accumulation plan. Retirement income isn't even part of the equation."

"The Benefits Policy Statement's first and primary goal for core retirement plans we would suggest is that it's formally stated that the primary purpose is to provide retirement income for life for the participant. With that guidepost, everything changes with regard to plan design."

Next Steps for Plan Design

Now that the committee is taking the time to lay out and build the foundation for the program, it's a good time to consider adding a trusted partner to the team -- a retirement plan specialist. This specialist is not only a specialist to call upon for assistance in designing and implementing the plan, but is also a fiduciary that will have as much "skin in the game" as the committee for the ongoing objective of helping participants achieve successful outcomes.

[2] Rod Crane's complete comments can be viewed at http://investingforcatholics.com/films/rod-crane-tiaa-cref.aspx. A sample Benefits Policy Statement provided by TIAA-CREF is available at http://investingforcatholics.com/plan_governance/.

Chapter 5

Our Trusted Partners

"Fee transparency" - the latest buzz words in the retirement plan industry. With this transparency has come increased fiduciary responsibility for plan sponsors.

Under new regulations (the ERISA 408(b) (2) disclosure rule), it is incumbent upon sponsors to understand the specific fees paid for plan services and sign off on the reasonableness of those fees. Plan sponsors are also required to pass this information on to the participants and, as a fiduciary, plan sponsors should ensure that the fees participants pay under the retirement plan are "reasonable" for the services received. As the focus on fees has increased, people are starting to pay attention, particularly to the fees charged for investments.

Why the focus on fees? Quite simply, according to fi360, this has been an area of significant perceived abuse, and it has a substantial impact on participant ending wealth. Though service providers have long been required to disclose fees to participants, much of the information was obscured in opaque disclosures. Many plan sponsors and the majority of participants have been unaware of "hidden fees." One impact of the new regulations is that plan sponsors are becoming far more educated. They are starting to ask explicitly tough questions about how their providers get paid. And they are coming face to face with another layer of the complexity and liabilities of their fiduciary role: fee disclosure makes it easier to measure the impact of fees so judges, juries and arbitration panels can come up with reasonable estimates of damage if awards for breaches of fiduciary responsibilities are deemed to be appropriate.

The bright spot is that most plan sponsors operate their plans without penalties or lawsuits. To make sure your plan is among them, make sure you build a foundation of prudent processes by adopting ERISA standards and creating a Benefits Policy Statement (BPS). But the real key to having a successful plan goes beyond the goals and objectives documented in the BPS and even beyond the intricacies of fee disclosure – and that key is the realization that the fiduciary role of the plan sponsor is not a do-it-yourself proposition. It is imperative to delegate tasks to trusted partners who are not only professional providers with subject matter expertise, but also can commit to taking on real fiduciary responsibility and accountability for your retirement program.

Quality Professional Providers

In seeking professional providers, you are looking for true trusted partners in the sense of *fiduciarius*, the Latin adjective that means "holding on trust; held on trust." Your organization should not settle for one of the historically opaque and higher-cost "bundled" plans that provide the so-called convenience of one-stop-shopping, but little if any fiduciary protection. Nor should you accept incoherent, incomplete or confusing answers to questions about fee structure or the level of fiduciary responsibility a given provider is willing to assume –

especially if they tell you that you don't need to worry about it because you have a non-ERISA plan. And finally, the committee does not need to be "sold" a plan where the provider underestimates the importance of a fiduciary committment because they cannot or will not accept fiduciary delegation.

When looking to outsource plan administration, plan sponsors are often confused about whether they should go with "bundled" or "unbundled" services. There are primarily five service components to retirement plans: recordkeeping, administration, asset custody, investments, and education. The bundled model is where one single vendor provides all service components with an "all in" fee structure that may be difficult to understand and is usually coupled with limited fiduciary responsibility. The unbundled model offers the flexibility to delegate fiduciary responsibilities and to select the best provider for each service component in an open architecture environment with complete fee transparency.

We believe that the best model for hiring trusted partners is for the plan sponsor to become its own "bundler" and to adopt a version of an "unbundled" plan that combines what is known as a 3(38) Investment Management fiduciary with a highly rated service provider that can provide the remaining recordkeeping, administration, asset custody, and education services.

Dimensional Fund Advisors' Vice President Apollo Lepescu has created a comprehensive comparison chart for Old Style (i.e., bundled) versus Modern (i.e., unbundled) plans:

RETIREMENT PLAN:	OLD STYLE (BUNDLED)	MODERN (UNBUNDLED)
Business model	Opaque, bundled offering that might lead to conflicts of interest	Independent, open architecture and full transparency
Assistance with plan administration and design	Limited flexibility in the plan design and selection of providers	Identification of optimal partners; custom plan design and administration
Services for plan participants	Inconsistent, and in many cases non-existent	Mutually agreed-upon service plan custom-tailored to plan's needs
ERISA fiduciary risk management	Limited scope, or no stated fiduciary responsibility	Assume fiduciary responsibility, no conflict of interest, and full disclosure

Fiduciary Classifications

Because terms like fiduciary, trustee, plan administrator and custodian seem to be used almost interchangeably at times and can be confusing – and also because we still don't want to install the doors and windows into our structure before the foundation is set - it is helpful to start with a clarification of the various fiduciary roles for qualified retirement plans that are spelled out in ERISA. The information below is derived, in large part, from 401khelpcenter.com, and explains the different types and scopes of fiduciaries:

Named Fiduciary - Always considered to be a fiduciary within the meaning of ERISA section 3(21), this is the responsible party named in the plan documents with the duty and the power under ERISA to operate the plan.

- Sometimes referred to as a "full scope" 3(21) fiduciary
- An investment advisor is not the full scope 3(21) fiduciary unless the advisor is the Named Fiduciary with authority to hire, monitor, fire and replace service providers and other fiduciaries

Plan Administrator - Defined in section 3(16) of ERISA and should not be confused with a "pension administrator" or a "Third Party Administrator"

- The Plan Administrator ensures that all filings with the federal government are made; makes disclosures to plan participants; hires plan service providers; and fulfills other responsibilities as set forth in plan documents

Trustee - Defined in sections 403(a) and 403(b) of ERISA. The Trustee is a person or group of persons recognized as having exclusive authority and discretion over the management and control of plan assets.

- These duties are distinct from those of the Named Fiduciary who has the duty to control, manage and administer the plan, but the Named Fiduciary can also serve as the Trustee
- When the Trustee is a separate person, the Trustee is accountable to and monitored by the Named Fiduciary
- The Named Fiduciary can appoint an ERISA 3(38) Investment Manager to provide directions to the Trustee

3(38) Investment Manager – Defined under ERISA section 3(38) as a fiduciary with full discretionary powers for selecting, monitoring and/or replacing the investment options in a qualified plan. When the 3(38) is appointed by the Named Fiduciary:

- The Trustee becomes "directed" by the 3(38)
- The Named Fiduciary has responsibility for monitoring the 3(38)
- The 3(38) must ensure that the objectives of the plan's portfolios are being met in accordance with the Investment Policy Statement (IPS)

- INVESTMENT ADVISOR – Not a term defined by ERISA in the same manner as the other fiduciaries, the Investment Advisor usually does not have discretion over plan assets and is often referred to as limited-scope 3(21) fiduciary.
  - "These limited scope ERISA §3(21) fiduciaries have limited scope because they have limited decision making because the buck still remains with the plan sponsor," says Ary Rosenbaum, of The Rosenbaum Law Firm P.C. [1]

- Others that act with discretion or authority "to any extent" – Includes members of the committee as well as anyone that may be acting in a fiduciary capacity under ERISA based on their actions.
  - The committee may collectively serve as the Named Fiduciary and/or Trustee, but the committee generally serves as a council and reports to the Named Fiduciary and Trustee
  - The committee may be entrusted by the Named Fiduciary with monitoring other fiduciaries such as the 3(38) Investment Advisor

As you can see, there are significant differences among the fiduciary levels, particularly between a limited scope 3(21) investment advisor

[1] http://www.jdsupra.com/legalnews/breaking-the-code-of-erisa-fiduciaries-49519/

and a 3(38) Investment Manager. That is why the plan sponsors should carefully ensure that they are partnered with a 3(38). As fiduciaries to the Plan, they do more than talk about the concepts of fiduciary responsibility; they live it and have skin in the game.

Benefits of Delegation

Delegating fiduciary responsibilities to a 3(38) Investment Manager puts investment selection and oversight into the hands of an expert with enhanced skills and resources who takes on legal responsibility for investment decisions.

In addition, the 3(38) consults as a subject matter expert and also frees up the plan sponsor to focus on the myriad other activities associated with operating the plan.

In exchange, the Plan Sponsor remains responsible for monitoring the 3(38)'s process and costs to ensure they are in the best interests of the plan and the participants. The Employee Benefits Security Administration (EBSA), an agency of the Department of Labor (DOL) has published a thoughtful brochure called "Meeting Your Fiduciary Responsibilities" that outlines key information with regard to monitoring service providers:

> *An employer should establish and follow a formal review process at reasonable intervals to decide if it wants to continue using the current service providers or look for replacements. When monitoring service providers, actions to ensure they are performing the agreed-upon services include:*

- *Reviewing the service providers' process and performance;*
- *Reading any reports they provide;*
- *Checking actual fees charged;*
- *Asking about policies and practices (such as trading, investment turnover, and proxy voting); and*
- *Following up on participant complaints.* [2]

10 POINTS FOR VETTING AN ADVISOR

When vetting a fiduciary for your program, the candidates should answer the following quesitons in writing:

- Are you a 3(38) Fiduciary as defined by ERISA?
- Will you accept responsiblity for selecting investment options?
- Will you accept responsibility for monitoring investment options?
- Will you accept responsibility for replacing investment options?
- Will you act solely in the best interest of plan participants?
- Will you acknowledge, in writing, your ability and willingness to accept the delgation of fiduciary responsibility?
- Will you agree to accept no payment from plan investments?
- Do you have an ERISA bond that specifically cites that you are a 3(38) Investment Manager?

[2] http://www.dol.gov/ebsa/publications/fiduciaryresponsibility.html

- Has your organization ever been sued for breach of fiduciary responsibility, whether the suit was settled out of court or not?

- Bonus question: do you hold any fiduciary designations such as the fi360 AIF or AIFA?

Vetting a Plan Service Provider

In addition to delegating investment management to a 3(38), careful consideration must also be given to the day-to-day operations of administering the plan. The committee will want to work with quality providers to ensure that the plan is managed and operated in accordance with the plan document. And while fees are important, it is important to remember that a focus solely on the lowest possible fee may be at the cost of successful employee outcomes or other quality services that you need to manage your plan.

With regard to fees, the EBSA writes:

> *Fees are just one of several factors fiduciaries need to consider in deciding on service providers and plan investments. When the fees for services are paid out of plan assets, fiduciaries will want to understand the fees and expenses charged and the services provided. While the law does not specify a permissible level of fees, it does require that fees charged to a plan be "reasonable." After careful evaluation during the initial selection, the plan's fees and expenses should be monitored to determine whether they continue to be reasonable.*
>
> *In comparing estimates from prospective service providers, ask which services are covered for the estimated fees and which are not. Some providers offer a number of services for one fee, sometimes referred to as a "bundled" services arrangement. Others charge separately for individual services. Compare all services to be provided with the total*

> *cost for each provider. Consider whether the estimate includes services you did not specify or want. Remember, all services have costs.* [3]

When you are searching for a quality plan service provider, the EBSA recommends for documentation purposes that you "provide each of them with complete and identical information about the plan and what services you are looking for so that you can make a meaningful comparison."

The EBSA goes on to say:

> *For a service contract or arrangement to be reasonable, service providers must provide certain information to you about the services they will provide to your plan and all of the compensation they will receive. This information will assist you in understanding the services, assessing the reasonableness of the compensation (direct and indirect), and determining any conflicts of interest that may impact the service provider's performance.*

In our experience, the most important attribute of any service provider is that they will partner with you to develop strategies designed to meet your organization's goals and objectives for a successful outcome for your plan participants. To that end, you will want to make sure you speak the same language and you will want to know:

- Does the provider have experience with the type of plan offered by your organization?

- Does the provider have a robust "back office" management system for uploading census data, depositing contributions and loan payments, tracking distributions, etc. — and can you request on-the-fly management reports as needed?

---

[3] http://www.dol.gov/ebsa/publications/fiduciaryresponsibility.html

- Does the provider have a robust "client facing" website that focuses on educating the client about their account and preparing them for retirement?

You will want to evaluate all of this documentation carefully because, as Ary Rosenbaum observes, "there is nothing worse than buying a service that really isn't what it says it is."

NEXT STEPS

With outsourcing fiduciary tasks to professional fiduciaries and subject matter specialists, the committee will be able to delegate certain fiduciary responsibilities and also add an enhanced level of expertise, accountability and oversight to daily operations. With your foundation thus strengthened, your trusted partners will serve as a resource to help you build the framework of your plan design with a purpose, as we will discuss in the next chapter.

Chapter 6

Our Plan Design with a Purpose

As Americans continue to grapple with a challenging economy, their confidence in their ability to retire comfortably remains at a historically low level, according to the 2013 Retirement Confidence Survey conducted by the Employee Benefits Research Institute (EBRI). Saving for retirement often comes in third place after dealing with the daily cost of living and managing debt. Workers – including those who are actively saving for retirement – have no clear idea of how much they actually need to save. The savings and investment process required to prepare for retirement intimidates most workers.

Your organization is also likely dealing with challenges of the post-Great Recession economy and may be in the throes of making changes to the retirement program as a result – changes that ask participants to take more responsibility for their own retirement savings. With these changes, it's natural for your participants to look to you as plan sponsor for guidance with structuring their retirement strategy – and, by embracing "plan design with a purpose," your organization can be a genuine source of assistance.

"Sponsors that follow a prudent due diligence process in plan design, combined with effective education communicated in a strategic manner, may influence participant behavior, thus enabling them to save and invest for a more financially secure retirement," writes Shlomo Benartzi of the UCLA Andersen School of Management in *Save More Tomorrow*.

"Plan design with a purpose" makes an explicit effort to guide participant behavior toward positive outcomes. The goal is to implement a plan that works for participants by helping them achieve a level of savings that will produce an adequate income in retirement, and:

- Encourages enrollment and adequate contribution levels
- Provides genuine advice, beyond guidance, that drives action and outcomes
- Offers accessible, streamlined participant communication
- Includes target date investments
- Monitors progress toward retirement readiness and sets benchmarks for success

According to the Department of Labor, approximately 30% of eligible workers do not participate in their employer's plan.[1] However, plan sponsors can boost the possibility of retirement plan success by making it easier for participants to enroll and keep their money in the plan, increase their contributions, allocate their investments, and generate a steady stream of lifetime income. How?

[1] http://www.dol.gov/ebsa/publications/automaticenrollment401kplans.html

"Better plan design would have an (almost) immediate impact in helping participants save for retirement," writes Tim Kohn, Head of DC Services, Dimensional Fund Advisors, in an article exploring the results of the EBRI 2013 survey in "DC Dimensions" (Summer 2013).

Better plan design starts with a look back at the impacts on plan sponsors and participants of the movement away from Defined Benefit (DB) plans toward Defined Contribution (DC) retirement plans. These impacts are driving a change in thinking about what a DC retirement plan is all about. For decades, the DC plan industry and its providers have focused on asset accumulation, leading participants to lose focus on how asset accumulation leads to retirement income. As a result, there is growing interest in making certain aspects of DC plans function more like DB plans — leading to developments such as automatic enrollment, automatic escalation and employer contributions.

Step 1: Automatic Enrollment

According to the DOL, studies suggest that automatic enrollment could reduce the 30% non-participation rate in most DC plans to less than 15%, significantly increasing retirement savings.

Further studies show that auto enrollment is not enough by itself to keep participants on the path to a secure retirement. The key is to implement the ***right*** initial default contribution rate – in short, plan design with a purpose.

In their book *Nudge: Improving Decisions About Health, Wealth and Happiness*, authors Richard Thaler and Cass Sunstein note that automatic enrollment programs do work, but plan sponsors have typically adopted a relatively low default savings rate of 2% or 3%. As it turns out, many participants continue saving at that default rate — which is far too low to provide enough money for retirement.

According to Benartzi (in *Save More Tomorrow*), participants may in fact take a default rate as tacit advice, and simply stay with it. Inertia traps people into continuing to do what they are currently doing, rather than changing their behavior. However, plan sponsors can help participants use inertia to their advantage by considering a higher initial default contribution rate of 4% to 6%, and let participants opt out if they feel their compensation does not permit that rate.

In fact, in his article on the EBRI 2013 Retirement Confidence Survey, Dimensional's Tim Kohn writes:

> *The 2006 Pension Protection Act green-lighted automatic enrollment, so we asked workers how they would feel about automatic enrollment at both a 3% and 6% deferral rate. Among workers automatically enrolled into a retirement plan, the survey found only 2 in 10 would opt out, with 77% continuing in the plan at a 3% rate, at a lower rate, or even at a higher rate.*
>
> *We subsequently asked workers to think about a 6% savings rate, and only 3 in 10 said they would opt out. Two-thirds of workers would continue to contribute at a 6% rate - and some at a decreased rate or at a rate exceeding 6%.*

The power of "opting out" – as opposed to volunteering to save for retirement – is one of the keys to plan design success."[2]

Step 2: Automatic Escalation

An annual retirement savings rate in the range of 10% to 15% is generally thought to be the optimal level required to create adequate savings for retirement income. Supplementing the initial automatic enrollment default rate with an automatic annual increase – i.e., automatic escalation - will help participants achieve their optimal savings rate.

When adding an automatic increase, consider a level of, say, 4%, instead of the 2-3% generally used. Tim Kohn writes that "Combining both automatic enrollment and automatic escalation beyond the industry norm of 3% can and will impact the savings rates for workers. We know of no better immediate change in plan design that can effectively capitalize on inertia and start workers on the path to saving for a better retirement."

Step 3: Integrate an Employer Contribution

Offering an employer contribution will give participants another boost for reaching their optimal savings rate. Some organizations prefer to make a "flat" contribution regardless of the amount participants choose to contribute – particularly those organizations that have previously offered DB plans. The argument is that the participants will have at least some level of savings for retirement even if they otherwise choose to opt out of the plan.

On the other hand, integrating part or all of this contribution as an employer match can serve to enhance participation and maximize employee contributions. To encourage employees to contribute as much as they can, offer a clear and simple formula. Note that

[2] DC Dimension, Summer 2013, *Let Plan Design Show Us the Way*

participants will consider a match as "free money," which they will be reluctant to lose if they don't contribute. Matches are generally contributed up to a salary cap – such as matching 100% of contributions up to 4% of salary.

Note that participants will tend to interpret the salary cap as a signal of how much they should save, but will have a strong incentive to contribute up to the amount matched nonetheless. If an employer matches a given percent of contributions ("A" – the match) up to a maximum percent of salary ("B" – the salary cap), "B" affects behavior more than "A." Employers should consider increasing the salary cap ("B") while proportionately reducing the match ("A") to keep costs the same. For an example, instead of matching 100% of worker contributions up to 4% of salary, match 50% on the first 8% contributed. This will result in a higher level of employee contributions while not increasing the amount you pay.

A Note about Loans

To reinforce for employees the concept that participating in the plan represents a commitment to long-term retirement planning rather than as a source of funds during the accumulation years, consider placing limits on the number of loans participants can take against their retirement assets. While they may sometimes be necessary, loans are inconsistent with the objectives of the plan.

Although participants are required to pay them back with interest, loans represent funds that are taken out of the market, which can have a significantly negative effect on long-term asset growth. In addition, the fees charged for taking out a loan further decrease the asset accumulation intended for retirement.

Limiting loans to no more than one at a time is advisable. Further, loans should be taken only from participant contributions rather than plan sponsor additions.

Next Steps

As we discussed in Chapter 2, the fi360 handbook breaks the fiduciary process down into a series of practices that follow a simple four-step "fiduciary quality management system": Organize; Formalize; Implement; and Monitor. Now that we are reaching Step 3: Implement, it is likely that because your organization has one or more plans already in place, you are wondering how to change, replace, migrate or bundle them into a new one. You will find that open, honest discussion with your trusted advisors will help you implement an integrated plan design.

As your discussions progress, please bear in mind that in addition to the three key considerations in implementing plan design - plan features, the investment menu, and the service model – it is also essential that your participants engage with the plan. In this chapter, we focused on building the structure of our plan design with a purpose. In the next chapter, we will examine how to effectively communicate this plan to your participants.

Chapter 7

Our Message for Participants

Behavioral economists have identified some key reasons why participants may become intimidated by the decision making processes required to prepare for retirement and may not fully engage with their retirement plan:

- **Present Bias:** As Shlomo Benartzi writes in *Save More Tomorrow*, this bias is the tendency to sharply reduce the importance of the future in decision making. People greatly prefer to spend now rather than save for the future. They are seduced into believing that doing the right thing in the future would be easier (i.e., less painful) than it is now. They end up procrastinating.

- **Procrastination Leads to Inertia:** Despite good intentions, individuals fail to act. The savings and investment process required to prepare for retirement intimidates most individuals leading to inertia. Inertia is why workers fail to enroll when offered a chance to participate in a Defined Contribution (DC) plan.

- **Choice Overload:** If some choice is good, it might appear that more choice is better, but this approach can be counterproductive. Individuals can be overwhelmed with too much information or too much choice. They may put off making a choice altogether or simply pick the first thing on a list.

As we discussed in the last chapter, effective plan design is critical to delivering positive participant results. Automatic enrollment is a design element which is being embraced more widely by plan sponsors as it has been shown to successfully increase plan participation.

With this change in how the industry and plan sponsors approach plan design has come another realization – that patterns of behavior can present barriers that prevent participants from fully understanding and engaging with retirement plans.

Targeted Participant Education

In choosing your service provider, you will want to ensure that they will work with you to overcome behavioral barriers by providing targeted participant education, including:

- Online access to robust account information that includes:
  - Automated enrollment with simple steps
  - A snapshot view of account status
  - Benefit statements that project the stream of income that can be expected at retirement
  - Interactive tools to gauge retirement readiness

Targeted Benefit Statements

Your service provider should be able to support all of your goals for online access and targeted benefit statements.

While a retirement income calculation is not yet required on benefit statements by ERISA, there are service providers that currently provide this information. In addition, the Department of Labor in 2013 announced that new rules to that effect are being considered. According to an "Advanced Notice of Proposed Rule Making" (ANPRM) posted in The Federal Register – The Daily Journal of the United States Government, the DOL "believes that expressing a participant's current and projected account balances as lifetime income streams would allow participants to make more informed retirement planning decisions."

The DOL has made available an online interactive calculator that calculates lifetime income streams in accordance with the proposed regulatory framework. This calculator is found at: www.dol.gov/ebsa/regs/lifetimeincomecalculator.html. Also, a comprehensive retirement analyzer tool can be found at www.investingforcatholics.com.

Paradigm Shift

Because households have unique economic characteristics that directly affect the calculation of income replacement needs at retirement, your 3(38) Investment Manager as well as your service vendor should be able to provide a number of up-to-date assessment tools to help participants determine their unique savings rate.

Marlena I. Lee, vice president, Dimensional Fund Advisors, said in the Summer 2012 issue of *DC Dimensions* that "plan sponsors should remain vigilant about improving their plans. As we look to the next generation of retirement plans, it's important to move the paradigm from savings to consumption planning."

Income needs in retirement are based on individual spending habits, according to a study conducted by Lee. This study found that:

> *Replacement rates can differ substantially across households depending on individual retirement goals, tax rates, and accumulated savings. Using pre-retirement income as a sorting variable, we obtain income replacement rates that range from 58% for highly compensated employees to about 82% for low-wage earners.*
>
> *For plan sponsors, understanding what replacement rate is appropriate for participants is critical in assessing a plan's adequacy. Benchmarking retirement plans without controlling for participant characteristics might lead to faulty conclusions about retirement readiness.*

The wide variance in replacement rates comes about when studying the spending habits of households, not just current income. This approach is not one-size-fits-all and more often than not requires the touch of your 3(38) who can provide individualized advice.

Next Steps

Because the committee "knows" the participants in your organization, you will want to work closely with your 3(38) Investment Manager to find a service provider that can provide the array of communications materials and other types of support needed to help your participants achieve retirement plan success.

It is important to note that one of the most crucial aspects of participant communication is helping participants understand their investment options. This aspect of your communication efforts will be informed by your Investment Policy Statement, which will be examined in the next chapter.

Chapter 8

Our Investment Policy

In choosing to follow ERISA standards, you have adopted the premier level of fiduciary accountability for your organization's retirement plan, making it prudent to adopt an Investment Policy Statement (IPS). In fact, the importance of the IPS cannot be overstated. It will serve as the committee's guidepost for making fund decisions as well as for monitoring your service providers and Investment Manager for benchmarking results.

It will also serve as a communication piece for your plan participants – a doorway, if you will, into one of the most essential elements of their retirement plan success, which is the allocation of their investments. The IPS will help you assure that the plan gives your participants investment choices that will lead them toward meeting their goals.

As the committee creates the IPS, you will outline all of your essential goals and objectives regarding plan investments. The development of the IPS is both a learning and a communication process where, in close collaboration with your 3(38) Investment Manager and service provider, the committee will discover and outline your parameters for investment choices and then document the prudent processes you prefer for selection and monitoring. Your Investment Manager and service provider will help you ensure that your fiduciary obligations are being met.

It is important to note that while plan sponsors are not likely to be held accountable for not having the "highest-performing" funds, they are held accountable if they do not have a prudent investment policy in place or have one but are not following it. When auditing an ERISA plan, the Department of Labor regularly asks to review the procedures in place for reviewing plan investments. The existence of an IPS provides evidence of a prudent investment decision making process[1].

The IPS will generally include:

- Overview – describes the purpose of the plan (i.e., its "mission statement")
- Statement of Purpose – defines the overall purpose of the IPS with a timeline to regularly review it and also establishes the ability of the committee to update the IPS if necessary
- ERISA 404(c) – discloses that the Plan intends to be 404(c) compliant and outlines how it will meet those requirements (discussed further below)
- Statement of Objectives – outlines objectives for participant education which are essential to retirement plan success
- Roles and Responsibilities – describes who is responsible for choosing, managing and/or monitoring the plan's investments

[1] *Creating an Investment Policy Statement*, Norman M. Boone & Linda S. Lubitz

- **Investment Menu Design** – discloses the parameters for the fund choices included on the plan's investment menu, including what asset classes are included and why, and a description of the Plan's Qualified Default Investment Option (QDIA)

- **Investment Monitoring** – outlines how the plan will evaluate and reevaluate the funds offered and the procedure to be followed if a fund does not meet the criteria

Although your service provider will likely supply a sample IPS with basic boilerplate language, it is a good idea to customize the document as much as possible to match the circumstances and needs of your organization's plan.

Overview

In this opening section of the IPS, the committee will establish the mission statement for the plan. The details will include the plan sponsor's intent to comply with ERISA regulations as well as a commitment to invest according to faith-based standards established by The United States Conference of Catholic Bishops (USCCB). The terms used in this section should parallel the same terms used and defined in the plan documents. A boilerplate sample (with contribution from TIAA-CREF) could look like this:

> The {name of the plan}, established by {name of your organization} (the Plan Sponsor), is intended to provide eligible employees the opportunity to generate the long-term accumulation of retirement savings through employer and employee contributions to individual Participant accounts and the earnings thereon. The Plan is an employee benefit plan intended to comply with the spirit of all applicable federal laws and regulations including the Internal Revenue Code of 1986, as amended, and the Employee Retirement Income Security Act of 1974 (ERISA), as amended.

The Plan is comprised of: a defined contribution plan; and {indicate here prior plans that have been frozen or amended – provide further description in an additional paragraph if needed}.

The Plan Sponsor appoints {name of your committee} (the Committee). The Committee shall supervise the investment of the assets of the plan and make all decisions concerning selection and retention of the investment options available under the plan. Accordingly, the Committee shall have authority both to select and monitor funds, and to appoint an Investment Manager that is qualified under ERISA to act as a fiduciary for the Plan. The Plan's investment funds will be selected and monitored with the skill, care and diligence that a prudent individual acting in a like capacity would undertake and in accordance with all other aspects of applicable law.

It is the intent of the Plan to provide a range of investment options that will enable Participants to invest according to varying risk tolerances, savings time horizons, and other financial goals.

These investment options shall be consistent with the Socially Responsible Investment Guidelines as provided by The United States Conference of Catholic Bishops. These guidelines will be updated from time to time and currently include:

- Protecting human life
- Promoting human dignity
- Reducing arms production
- Pursuing economic justice
- Protecting the environment
- Encouraging corporate responsibility

Statement of Purpose

This section describes the intention of the IPS itself and is sometimes included within the Overview. Sample language may look like this:

The purpose of this document is to provide the Committee with guidance when making decisions concerning the Plan's investment funds, including effectively structuring an appropriate investment menu and establishing a prudent process for selecting, monitoring and, as necessary, replacing funding options.

This IPS shall be reviewed at least annually by the Committee, and the Committee may, from time to time as warranted, modify the objectives and criteria as it deems appropriate.

ERISA 404(c) Rights and Obligations

Compliance with ERISA Section 404(c) is not mandatory for any plan, but by complying with the section's safe harbor guidelines, plan sponsors can reduce potential fiduciary risk. Soon after ERISA was enacted in 1974, the DOL issued regulatory guidance concerning general fiduciary duties, including requirements that plan fiduciaries diversify plan investments and choose investments in a prudent manner. In the early 1990's, the DOL issued further regulations under ERISA Section 404(c) that provide fiduciaries of defined contribution plans with some protection against liability for participant investment decisions, if certain conditions are met.

To comply, the employer must inform plan participants that they have control over their investments and that the Plan intends to comply with ERISA 404(c). Next, the Plan must offer at least three diversified "core" investment options representing a wide range of risk/return tolerances. These options typically include a money market fund, a bond fund and an equity fund. In practice, most new plans offer a more robust investment menu than this minimal number of investment options.

Additionally, participants must be able to make their own investment allocation decisions and have access to changing their investment selections at least once every three months at no more than a "reasonable" charge to the participant.

Finally, participants must receive sufficient information and education about the Plan's investment options so that they can make informed decisions.

Sample IPS language could look like this:

> The defined contribution Plan is intended to be maintained as an ERISA 404(c) Plan, as described in §404(c) of the Employee Retirement Income Security Act of 1974 ("ERISA"), and Title 29 of the Code of Federal Regulations Section 2550.404c-1. To do so, the general investment philosophy of the defined contribution Plan will be to provide Participants with a choice of broadly diversified lower-cost funds and blended portfolios that have different risk and return characteristics that match Participants' individual risk capacities and provide them with a corresponding expected investment return.
>
> Further, the defined contribution Plan will:
>
> - Provide Participants with a disclosure that the Plan is intended to be a 404(c) Plan within the meaning of ERISA Section 404(c) and that the Department of Labor regulations thereunder limit the Plan Fiduciaries' liability with respect to Participant-directed investments under the plan
>
> - Provide communication tools expressed in layman's terms to Participants to help them better understand investments and to help them identify their appropriate asset allocation.
>
> - Provide Participants with Target Date Portfolios comprised of globally diversified funds, enabling them to invest in accordance with their time horizon and risk capacity, or to create investment allocations of their own choosing
>
> - Generally allow Participants to change the investment direction of future deferrals and employer contributions

- Generally allow Participants to change the allocation of current account balances between the Target Date Portfolios and a personally designed allocation using the underlying funds

- Furnish Participants with necessary instructions to alter such investment allocations

- Furnish a fact sheet for each available fund under the Plan to eligible employees during their initial enrollment period, and thereafter upon request. Such descriptions shall be provided in a format designed to be understood by the average employee, and shall generally include the:
  - Fund's stated investment strategy
  - Fund's historical 1, 3, 5 and 10 year returns, when available, compared with an appropriate index

It is important to note that while compliance with the 404(c) rules may relieve plan fiduciaries of certain liability for losses resulting from investment decisions made by participants and beneficiaries, it does not relieve them of all fiduciary responsibilities concerning Plan investments. Fiduciaries must still prudently select the investment alternatives made available to participants and monitor the investment performance of these selections.

Statement of Objectives

In this section, the committee will set forth its objectives for participant education. Education is particularly important for participants in 404(c) compliant plans to successfully exercise their responsibilities for deferring and investing their individual accounts.

In developing a continued participant investment education program, the committee will want to remember, as Albert Einstein said, "Make everything as simple as possible, but not simpler." Funds and supporting materials should be selected with consideration for the following:

- The number of funds offered should be limited enough to promote participant understanding without sacrificing the objectives of the investment policy

- Participants should be encouraged to select an appropriate asset allocation (based on their risk tolerance, their time until retirement and other factors relating to their personal financial status) and avoid attempts to time the market

- Materials should educate participants on the relative risk and return of investing in different asset classes and how diversification can reduce the risk of investing

Boilerplate language for the IPS could look like this:

> The Plan will encourage Participants to take an active role for their retirement by providing education and information so that they can make informed decisions about their participation and funding option selections. The Plan's funding options will be selected to:
>
> - Provide returns comparable to the appropriate benchmark for the asset categories
> - Provide opportunities to diversify across the risk-return spectrum with a range of investment choices within varied asset classes
> - Control administrative, management and Participant costs
>
> A significant responsibility of the Plan is to ensure that adequate Participant education and communication are provided. The Committee will assess whether the quantity and quality of Participant education and communication is appropriate. Participant education can be achieved through a variety of channels, including printed materials, websites, group meetings and individual counseling.

Roles and Responsibilities

There are a variety of individuals and groups who may be deemed to be fiduciaries for your organization's plan. In this section of the IPS, the committee will want to identify the various parties exercising influence over the plan assets and delineate their responsibilities. The IPS may include language similar to the samples below:

The Plan Sponsor:

- Delegates investment fiduciary responsibilities to the Investment Committee
- Reviews and approves the IPS
- Avoids prohibited transactions and conflicts of interest

The Investment Committee:

- Establishes and maintains the IPS
- Controls and manages overall plan fees and expenses
- Monitors and supervises all service venders and the Investment Managers
- Generates communications to Participants when necessary

The Investment Manager:

- Follows the IPS
- Is qualified under ERISA to acts as a fiduciary to the Plan
- Exercises full investment discretion with regards to prudent selection, monitoring and removal/replacement of fund options
- Reviews and reports performance of investment options in accordance with frequencies required in the IPS against established peer groups and benchmarks

Service Provider:

As the Third Party Administrator (TPA)

Responsible for all documentation, administration, testing and reporting functions and requirements necessary to keep the Plan in compliance with all regulatory governing bodies, including but not limited to:

- Summary Annual Report generation
- Loan and distribution documentation and approval
- Document and Summary Plan Description (SPD) maintenance

As Recordkeeper

Responsible for maintaining daily values for all Participant accounts and to facilitate transactions originated by the Plan Sponsor or Participants such as contributions, transfers and distributions. The Recordkeeper's technology and personnel are primarily responsible for:

- Contribution processing
- Plan and Participant level reporting
- Certain website maintenance
- Investment trading and account reconciliation
- Distribution and Loan processing

As Custodian

Responsible for the safekeeping of the Plan's assets; the specific duties and responsibilities of the custodian are:

- Value the holdings
- Collect all income and dividends owed to the Plan
- Settle all transactions (buy-sell orders)
- Provide monthly reports that detail transactions, cash flows, securities held and their current value, and change in value of each security and the overall plan since the previous report
- Maintain separate accounts by legal registration

Investment Menu Design

One of the most complex processes involved in implementing and maintaining a retirement plan is the construction of the investment menu. As with all other responsibilities of the committee, a prudent process is essential.

Suffice it to say there are a number of assessment criteria to be used in selecting investment options for your organization's plan. You will want to discuss these with your 3(38) Investment Manager and your service provider. Those criteria agreed upon for the final selection will be the same criteria used for ongoing monitoring of the fund selections.

You may wish to summarize the list of final criteria in the IPS, and you may do so in this section. We will discuss the processes and criteria involved in detail in the next chapter. Short of that list of criteria, following is what boilerplate language for this section may look like:

> The Plan will offer a broad range of different asset categories recognizing different ranges of market capitalization. The asset categories selected are such that, when taken together, Participants have a reasonable opportunity to potentially realize investment returns in their accounts while at the same time controlling risk or volatility.
>
> While offering a variety of funding options is important, efforts will be made to keep the total number to a prudent level that balances the benefits of broad diversification with the disadvantages of too many choices. The funding options for the Plan are listed in Appendix A {note: this will be a simple list attached to the IPS}.
>
> Long-term investment performance, in large part, is primarily a function of asset class mix. Mutual funds representing indexes in the following general asset classes are offered in the Plan:
>
> - U.S. Large Cap
> - U.S. Small Cap
> - Real Estate Investment Trusts
> - International Developed
> - Emerging Markets
> - Fixed Income
>
> Investment performance (gross of fees) shall either (a) approximate or exceed relevant benchmarks or (b) be above the appropriate peer universe, in either case over three, five, or ten years. Annualized investment returns shall be compared to appropriate benchmarks.
>
> In the Defined Contribution Plan, each Target Date Portfolio is composed of allocations to a variety of the underlying funds with differing risk/return characteristics. The Target Date Portfolios are age-based, each with a different target maturity date to accommodate Plan Participants' various ages and anticipated retirement dates.

> The investment objective of the Target Date Portfolios is to provide a multi-asset-class funding solution that offers investment diversification incorporating an allocation that progresses from more aggressive to more conservative as the Participant approaches a given target retirement date. Specifically, the composition of each Target Date Portfolio is modified over time following a predetermined schedule, slowly adapting from a more aggressive allocation to an allocation that assumes less risk as the retirement date approaches.
>
> A periodic review of the Target Date Fund's asset allocation and rebalancing strategies will be undertaken to ensure the prudence of these processes. Consideration will also be given to the stability and continuity of the funds included in the Target Date offering.
>
> The Target Date Portfolios are designated as the default funding option in the Plan. These age appropriate funding options are intended to meet the requirements of the applicable Department of Labor (DOL) regulation on Qualified Default Investment Alternatives (QDIA), Section 2550.404c-5. The default option will be automatically selected upon Plan enrollment, however, Participants can choose to opt out and actively build a portfolio by selecting from the menu of investment options underlying the Plan. On an annual basis, each default option shall be reviewed to ensure it continues to be an appropriate default option.

When the committee updates the IPS by adding the investment objectives that serve as the fund selection/monitoring criteria, you may find that the descriptions use industry-specific terms that are not readily understood by the layman. You may include definitions of those terms in a glossary attached to the IPS for further clarity.

Investment Monitoring

The IPS should establish a periodic review process of fund performance and the continued appropriateness of the investment selections. The same criteria that were applied in the original selection of the investment menu should be applied on an ongoing basis. The goal is to monitor the performance of your plan investments with enough frequency to spot trends that may indicate a need for change. There are four basic elements associated with monitoring:

- Performance reports and audited financial statements
- Changes affecting funds
- Benchmarking and comparing fees
- Confirming that the policies and procedures outlined in the IPS have been followed

Boilerplate language for the IPS may look like this:

> The ongoing monitoring of investments will be a regular and disciplined process. While frequent change is neither expected nor desirable, the process of monitoring investment performance relative to specified guidelines is an on-going process.
>
> The designated Investment Manager will review periodically each fund's progress in meeting the Plan's investment objectives on a quarterly basis. The Committee will review the Plan's investment offerings and the Investment Manager's actions pertaining to investment options at least once per year. The Committee realizes that short-term fluctuations may cause variations in performance. The Committee intends that investment performance be evaluated from a long-term perspective.
>
> Investment options that consistently underperform in terms of risk and return will be carefully reviewed to determine if any action is warranted. Investment options that consistently under perform in terms of risk and return will be carefully reviewed to determine if any action is warranted.
>
> The designated Investment Manager will review the investment objectives and risk characteristics, historical performance, and expenses related to

each investment option made available under the Plan. Each option will be monitored on the basis of its compatibility with the Plan's objectives to ensure it satisfies the investment goals of the Plan, and facilitates the development of individual asset allocation strategies if desired by a Participant.

Generally, all funds are expected to perform as well as or better than their prescribed performance standards, net of fees. If the Investment Manager finds that funds have deviated from the criteria, it may decide to place a fund on "watch list," recommend a replacement fund, or remove the option. Once the decision to terminate an investment option is made, asset transfer and liquidation should be handled to the best advantage of the Plan using one of the following approaches:

- Remove and replace with an alternative fund and move existing assets directly to the alternative fund
- Freeze the assets managed by the terminated fund and direct new assets to a replacement fund
- Phase out the fund over a specific time period
- Continue the fund but add a directly competing fund
- Remove the fund and do not provide a replacement

Next Steps

When the IPS is completed, you may wish to add a signature section to the document to memorialize the initial date upon which it was adopted. The adoption date is usually the same date that the plan documents are signed.

As mentioned, crafting the IPS will be a collaborative effort between the committee, the 3(38) Investment Manager and the service provider. A great deal of time will be spent on constructing the investment menu itself. This crucial process will be examined in further detail in the next chapter.

Chapter 9

Our Investment Options

In the early days of Defined Contribution plans, many fiduciaries thought that they could maximize protection under ERISA by designing investment menus that used a more-is-more approach, according to 401khelpcenter.com. If one fund family was good, four or five additional families were even better. However, participants were overwhelmed by the task of evaluating and selecting from among so many choices.

As we have discussed, too many choices can lead to participant inertia and indecision, not to mention that an extensive investment menu will also require a more extensive monitoring process on the part of the plan sponsor. Too many options can lead participants to feel overwhelmed.

As the structure of retirement plan investment menus continued to evolve, the more-is-more approach gave way to less-is-more. Plan sponsors developed menus that offered a few fixed income options and a varity of stock funds.

Today, fiduciaries are being tasked not just with offering adequate choices, but actually improving participant outcomes, according to

401khelpcenter.com. The old approaches are no longer working. Both designs – the more-is-more and the less-is-more approaches – assumed that all participants could create their own portfolios, which as we have discussed is generally not the case. These approaches also failed to address the increasing utilization of automatic enrollment.

The key is to provide a simple menu, with basic building blocks of prudently selected funds that make it easy for participants to understand their options and make choices that make sense for them coupled with a strong communication and education program to help participants with their retirement readiness.

With this in mind, it is time to determine the prudent processes that will be used to select investment options for the defined contribution plan menu.

Prudent Investor Rule

As plan steward, the committee will find that a good starting place for investment selection is with the Prudent Investor Rule, also referred to as UPIA – the Uniform Prudent Investor Act.

The rule, published in 1992, was written as a guideline for the prudent management of trust assets and many states passed it into law. In California it passed into law in 1996 under the title "The Uniform Prudent Investor Act." This rule points out the value of Modern Portfolio Theory. It essentially tells trustees that index funds are the prudent way to invest trust assets. The rule acts as a legal road map for estate planning attorneys, trustees of all types of trusts, and investment advisors.

Five Principles of Prudence

- Sound diversification is fundamental to risk management and is therefore ordinarily required of trustees

- Risk and return are so directly related that trustees have a duty to analyze and make conscious decisions concerning the levels of risk appropriate to the purposes, distribution requirements, and other circumstances of the trusts they administer

- Trustees have a duty to avoid fees, transaction costs and other expenses that are not justified by the needs and realistic objectives of the trust's investment program

- The fiduciary duty of impartiality requires a balancing of the elements of return between production of current income and the protection of purchasing power

- Trustees may have a duty as well as the authority to delegate as prudent investors would.

It is our experience and firm belief that these goals can all be met most assuredly through the implementation of a diverse menu of lower cost passively managed funds, or index funds. Index funds are mutual funds that follow a set of rules of ownership that are held constant regardless of market conditions. An important characteristic of an index fund is that its rules of ownership are not based on a forecast of short-term events. The goal of index investing is to enable plan sponsors to implement lower-cost retirement portfolios with appropriate risk exposures.

The New Evolution of Investment Menu Design

Shlomo Benartzi tells us in *Save More Tomorrow* that 90% of workers have no appetite for active involvement in investing and would prefer to delegate that responsibility to professionals. Of the remainder, 9% would like to be involved, but not deeply so, and the final 1% are highly sophisticated and wish to be extensively involved. A prudent approach to menu construction should help ensure a more secure retirement for all participants — both the 90% who will require a simple investment solution and the 10% who will want a variety of choice so they can build their own asset allocation.

By incorporating behavioral finance with a menu of index funds, we arrive at the new evolution of investment menu design: age-based Target Date Portfolios crafted with funds with the option to build a personal portfolio from the underlying investment options.
The Target Date Portfolios are age-based and risk appropriate. These portfolios automatically provide participants with periodic rebalancing and reallocation as they approach retirement. In addition, as described in the chapter on the Investment Policy Statement, these portfolios are an appropriate Qualified Default Investment Option (QDIA) for the defined contribution plan when paired with automatic enrollment.

Participants who want a variety of choice can opt out of the Target Date Portfolio and create their own portfolio from among the underlying lower-cost funds. As we have discussed, one of the goals of the plan will be to provide appropriate educational materials to aid those participants who wish to build their own investment allocation to help them achieve retirement plan success.

Investment Selection

The committee's search for investment funds should include those that have demonstrated successful investment history. In selecting an investment fund, the due-diligence process should analyze funds in terms of:

- Investment performance track record and consistency of returns given the risks taken relative to funds in its peer group
- Alignment of fund investment philosophy and style with plan option objectives
- Competitiveness of investment management fees
- Compatibility with plan trading requirements
- An assessment of the likelihood of future investment success relative to other opportunities

The committee will incorporate the components of the due diligence process used to select mutual funds into the Investment Policy Statement. These same measurements will be used to monitor funds on an ongoing basis and will be determined through conversation and consultation between the investment committee, your 3(38) Investment Manager and your service provider. When measured in tiers, we recommend that the funds selected fall within the top 25% when using such factors such as:

3, 5 & 10-Year Annualized Return - The rate of return which when compounded produces a fund's total return during the period under observation.

3, 5 & 10-Year Annualized Standard Deviation - A statistical measurement of dispersion around an average, which, for a mutual fund, depicts how widely the returns varied over a certain period of time. When a fund has a high standard deviation, the predicted range of short-term performance is wide, implying greater volatility.

Sharpe Ratio - A risk-adjusted measure developed by Nobel Laureate William Sharpe. It is calculated by using standard deviation and excess return to determine reward per unit of risk, according to Morningstar, Inc. The higher the Sharpe Ratio, the better the fund's historical risk-adjusted performance. The Sharpe ratio is calculated for the past 36-month period by dividing a fund's annualized excess returns by the standard deviation of a fund's annualized excess returns.

Turnover - This is a measure of the fund's trading activity which is computed by taking the lesser of purchases or sales (excluding all securities with maturities of less than one year) and dividing by average monthly net assets. A turnover ratio of 100% or more does not necessarily suggest that all securities in the portfolio have been traded, according to Morningstar, Inc. In practical terms, the resulting percentage loosely represents the percentage of the portfolio's holdings that have changed over the past year.

Net Expense Ratio - The percentage of fund assets used to pay for operating expenses and management fees, including 12b-1 fees, administrative fees, and all other asset-based costs incurred by the fund, except brokerage costs. Fund expenses are reflected in the fund's NAV. Sales charges are not included in the expense ratio. The expense ratio for fund of funds is the aggregate expense ratio, defined as the sum of the sponsor's fees plus the estimated weighted average of the underlying funds' fees.

Manager Tenure - The number of years that the current manager has been managing the investment. In the case of a team, the longest manager tenure is used.

Geometric Average Market Cap - Geometric average of the total equity market value of companies in a fund, expressed in millions of dollars. It equals shares outstanding times the stock price.

Price-to-Book Ratio - The P/B ratio of a company is a ratio measuring a company's per-share market price to a company's per-share book value. The per-share book value is the value of a company's tangible assets divided by the number of its shares. This figure may not always represent the real value of a company because it excludes such intangible assets as patents and trademarks. A high P/B ratio indicates that the price of the stock exceeds the actual worth of the company's assets.

Total Number of Holdings - Number of separate securities held by the mutual fund.

For fixed income options, additional factors include:

- Credit Rating - An average credit quality for all of a fund's bond holdings, ranging from AAA (highest) on down. U.S. Government bonds carry the highest credit rating, while bonds issued by speculative or bankrupt companies usually carry the lowest credit ratings. Anything at or below BB is considered a high-yield or "junk" bond.

- Effective Duration - A measure of a fund's interest-rate sensitivity — the longer a fund's duration, the more sensitive the fund is to shifts in interest rates. Duration is determined by a formula that includes coupon rates and bond maturities. Small coupons tend to increase duration, while shorter maturities and higher coupons shorten duration. The relationship between funds with different durations is straightforward: A fund with a duration of 10 years is twice as volatile as a fund with a five-year duration.

A Word about Fund Fees

Mutual funds can include a number of fees from management fees to 12b-1 fees to front end or back end loads along with "annual operating expenses." The SEC provides detailed information on this subject at http://www.sec.gov/answers/mffees.htm.

As the plan steward, you will want to be aware of these fees in making your investment choices. Fund fees directly affect the performance of the mutual fund – and that will directly affect the returns (or lack thereof) your participants will achieve in their retirement accounts.
You will want to avoid loads and 12b-1 fees. As for the remaining fees, we have found that index funds do the best job of holding the line as compared to "actively managed" funds, which by their nature incur higher trading costs and management fees as they seek to maintain their returns and charge a fee for their "expertise" in doing so. When funds are segregated into tiers by measurement of their fees, we recommend that the funds chosen fall within the "lowest" 25%.

Next Steps

Now you may be wondering if you can craft a faith-based investment strategy and still comply with all the fiduciary requirements we have just discussed. The answer is a definite "yes" as we will discuss in the next chapter.

Chapter 10

Our Faith-Based Investment Considerations

Your organization's desire is to invest in accordance with the tenets of the Catholic faith as encourage by The United States Conference of Catholic Bishops (USCCB). The USCCB has established Socially Responsible Investment Guidelines, which can be found at http://www.usccb.org/about/financial-reporting/socially-responsible-investment-guidelines.cfm.

Socially Responsible Investing

Socially Responsible Investing (SRI) is any investment strategy which seeks to consider both financial return and social good. It includes all of the financial decision making processes that are a part of a prudent investment management approach, but it also includes the selection and management of investments based on ethical, moral, social and/or environmental concerns.

In the last chapter, we discussed your fiduciary responsibilities under the Prudent Investor Rule, also called the Uniform Prudent Investor Act (UPIA). Under UPIA, there are some specific situations that remove any uncertainty about whether SRI screens are appropriate.

According to fi360, they are clearly permitted when:

- Plan documents permit the use of SRI
- A reasonable person would deduce from the organization's mission that SRI would be adopted

The best policy for the committee as the plan fiduciary is to treat your SRI strategy as you would any due diligence process. Do sufficient research to identify that the proposed strategy is likely to be prudent, effective, and practical to implement and is regularly monitored to show that the intended results have been accomplished – that participants are experiencing competitive returns that will help them achieve retirement plan success while investing according to your organization's core values.

Socially Responsible Screens

Screening is the most widely practiced approach to SRI. An effective approach incorporates the screen into the fund construction process. Certain fund managers work with highly regarded providers of research analytics to effectively screen the funds that underlie the Target Date Portfolios using faith-based exclusions. Implementing these same screens for the investments in your plan will enable your participants to invest according to specific risk parameters which carry an expected return, while maintaining their inherent and steadfast convictions which place a premium on life, social justice and the avoidance of degrading and inhumane practices.

An example of specific screens includes:

- Companies that are engaged in the development or manufacture of abortifacients; own or operate acute-care hospitals or surgical centers; or own more than 20% of, or are majority-owned by, companies that meet the preceding criteria.

- Companies that derive at least 15% of revenues from; rental, sale or distribution of adult entertainment media products; ownership and/or operation of adult entertainment establishments and production of adult media products including movies, magazines, books, calendars and websites.

- Companies that derive at least 15% of revenue from the manufacture of alcoholic beverages, the supply of raw materials and other products necessary for the production of alcoholic beverages or the distribution of alcoholic beverages.

- Companies whose operations have had major recent controversies relating to child labor infractions in the US or abroad.

- Companies that derive identifiable revenues from the development or manufacture of contraceptives; or that own more than 20% of, or are majority-owned by, companies that develop or manufacture contraceptives.

- Companies that derive at least 20% of revenue from the production of goods used exclusively for gambling, such as slot machines; ownership and/or operation of casinos, racetracks, bingo parlors, or other betting establishments; or the provision of services in casinos that are fundamental to gambling operations, such as gambling technology.

- Companies that are involved in the production of anti-personnel landmines, anti-vehicle landmines, or the essential components of these products.

- Companies that derive at least 20% of revenue from the production and/or sale of military weapons or weapons systems; customized components for military weapons or weapons systems; or weapons of mass destruction, including nuclear weapons, nuclear weapons systems, and customized components thereof.

- Companies that conduct stem cell research with cells derived from human embryos or fetal tissue, use fetal cell lines in the development of vaccines and other biologics such as therapeutic proteins and gene therapy products, or develop or produce products for scientific research specifically on embryonic or fetal stem cells, such as technology that isolates or regulates the growth and proliferation of stem cells.

- Companies that conduct business in Sudan, including those that own assets in, have employees/facilities in, obtain goods/services from, or have distribution agreements in Sudan; that issue credits or loans to companies domiciled in Sudan; or provide goods/services to, or purchase goods or commercial paper issued by, the government of Sudan.

- Companies that derive at least 15% of revenue from the manufacture of tobacco products, production of raw materials and other products necessary for the production of tobacco products, or the distribution of tobacco products.

Expected Returns

As the fiduciary for your organization's retirement plan, you will be concerned that the screened portfolios comply under the Prudent Investor Rule, which mandates that fiduciaries apply the principle of diversification when constructing portfolios, which is the process of spreading an investment across multiple asset classes as well as within a single asset class in the portfolio. In fact, the remaining universe of investments after applying the SRI screens is significantly large enough to provide diversification. And while there are costs involved with screening and monitoring, we have found that the screened funds have achieved competitive returns when compared to appropriate benchmarks – returns that make us comfortable from our own fiduciary standpoint.

Next Steps

Once your organization has elected to include socially responsible investing criteria when selecting investment options, the next step will be to update the IPS to define the appropriately structured SRI strategies that are to be applied.

And finally – having followed all the steps outlined up to this point - you are in a position to implement the new retirement plan. Your last step is to put in place your process for governance, as we will discuss in the next chapter – Our Stewardship.

Chapter 11
Our Stewardship

We have previously described the design of the retirement plan itself as analogous to framing the walls of a house. We have further referenced the investment menu as the doorway to financial well-being. We can think of our faith-based investment considerations as our roof – the part of the structure that protects us from inclement weather. That leaves us with plan governance – the ongoing upkeep of our infrastructure.

Ongoing Prudent Processes

As plan steward, you will want to ensure that your internal retirement plan management processes are prudent as well as:

- Consistent – your Benefits Policy Statement, Investment Policy Statement and all other plan documents should be consistent with each other using the same defined terms as well as coordinating goals and objectives.

    - Ensure that the goals and objectives outlined in these documents are translated into process guidelines that can be followed to effectively monitor fiduciary requirements

- **Relevant** - Institute an ongoing review process to:
  - help clarify how well your plan is working in relation to your plan objectives and identify areas for improvement
  - provide an opportunity for you and any advisor you may be working with to determine whether your plan objectives are still relevant
- **Efficient** – management of the retirement plan will likely include various departments and entities throughout your organization and it is most efficient to appoint an internal point person to:
  - create and manage internal administrative processes to include a calendar of committee deadlines – monthly, quarterly and annually
  - coordinate enrollment
  - oversee document management and retention (i.e. filing)
  - create checklists for ongoing processes and have staff use them ***every time***
  - retrieve management reports, such as those needed to monitor the 3(38) Investment Manager or to monitor plan participation
  - manage projects for plan service implementation within your HR and benefits teams as well as the IT environment
  - consolidate duplicative payroll processes

- **Vigilant** – you will want to stay abreast of changes that are taking place in the retirement plan landscape as well as within and outside your organization to ensure that the retirement plan continues to be well-positioned for participant success and aligns with fiduciary responsibility. New concepts and proposed regulations are reported in the news daily and your 3(38) Investment Advisor as well as your service provider should help you stay abreast of important changes to help you make sure your plan is properly aligned.

    - As this book was being written, Quinn Curtis, Associate Professor of Law, University of Virginia School of Law, and Ian Ayres, William K. Townsend Professor, Yale Law School, were completing their study called "Measuring Fiduciary and Investor Losses in 401(k) Plans." This is the first study of its type to take a look at the costs associated with fund choices in 401(k) plans by separating those costs into those attributable to investor behavior as compared to those attributable to fiduciaries (the architects of the investment menu). This study has generated lively conversation, and in part confirms that costs can be lowered by offering index funds.

Final Steps

At the end of the day, you will want to ensure that you are comfortable that the administration of the plan follows prudent processes that are focused on meeting your fiduciary and plan participant needs. It will be a coordinated effort, but one which should allow you to observe, in the words of Mother Theresa, that "I can do things that you cannot; you can do things that I cannot; but together we can do great things."

Chapter 12

Our Peace of Mind

Your organization is distinct and has its own history of retirement plans that have been offered or are currently in place for your participants, with their own inherent complexities. And though your circumstances are unique, you share a common heritage with all Catholic organizations that part of your mission is to help your workers achieve a secure retirement. It is also likely that your organization is at a crossroads with regard to your organization's retirement plan. Something needs to change, and we have walked with you throughout this book to show you how you can build a new secure retirement plan structure:

- Our Role - as fiduciaries, we as the committee serve as the cornerstone of the retirement plan
- Our Job – we act as a team and entertain a diversity of ideas to ensure that our cornerstone remains firmly in place
- Our Path – we lay out our foundation by determining where we are going and what our goals and options are for the retirement plan
- Our Trusted Partners – we build and strengthen our foundation by seeking out trusted partners - a professional plan service provider and a 3(38) Investment Manager who acts as a member of our team as a fiduciary with skin in the game

- **Our Plan Design with a Purpose** – we frame out the walls of our structure with a plan designed to encourage retirement plan participation through automatic enrollment
- **Our Message for Participants** – we open windows into their future by showing our participants how to achieve successful outcomes through participation in the retirement plan
- **Our Investment Policy** – we build a doorway to help our participants achieve successful retirement plan investing
- **Our Investment Options** – we strengthen the doorway with risk appropriate index fund options and age-based Target Date Portfolios
- **Our Faith-Based Investment Considerations** – we add a roof to our structure by screening the investment options to ensure that they align with our inherent core beliefs
- **Our Stewardship** – we make sure our infrastructure is in good order through the maintenance of prudent processes

Shepherding Your Plan

We wrote this book to lead you as commited Catholics to a sense of serenity from having arrived at this place where your house and your retirement plans are in order. Our hope is that you have been afforded some much needed clarity about the process, purpose and merits of a well-run retirement plan, and that you have freed up time to focus on the greater mission of your organization as well as on your family and community.

In a recent conversation with a CFO of a diocese, he confessed that his plan doesn't even have an Investment Policy Statement. We let him know that we are putting together this book about the best practices he might choose to apply. His response was, "When can I get that book. I need it now."

The good news for you is that these best practices are in your hands and you can start applying them today. If you take away nothing else from this handbook, please know this:

- It is imperative that you protect yourself and your participants by making sure you bring on board trusted partners that will accept fiduciary responsibility in writing

- Your participants can invest according to faith-based principles in an efficient, effective and prudent way that will also generate competitive returns for in their retirement accounts

- These best practices are designed to help you implement a plan that will bring you as a plan sponsor greater fiduciary protection and lead your participants to a better outcome

As committed Catholics, we wrote this book to lead you to a sense of serenity from having arrived at this place where your house and your retirement plans are in order. Our hope is that you have been afforded some much-needed clarity about the process, purpose and merits of a well-run church retirement plan. Doing so will ideally lead to the freeing up of your time to focus on the greater mission of our organization as well as on our family and community.

Glossary of Terms

401(k) Plan - In this type of defined contribution plan, the employee can make contributions from his or her paycheck before taxes are taken out. The contributions go into a 401(k) account, with the employee often choosing the investments based on options provided under the plan. In some plans, the employer also makes contributions, matching the employees' contributions up to a certain percentage.

Automatic Enrollment - Employers can automatically enroll employees in a plan and place contributions deducted from employees' paychecks into certain predetermined investments, unless the employees decide otherwise. Participants have the opportunity to opt out of participation and periodic opportunities to change their investments.

Benefit Accrual - The amount of benefits accumulated under the plan.

Benefit Statement - An individual benefit statement provides information about a participant's retirement benefits, such as the total plan benefits earned and vested benefits, on a periodic basis. Additional information may be included depending upon the type of plan, such as how a participant's plan account is invested and the value of those investments.

Defined Benefit Plan (DB Plan) - This type of plan, also known as the traditional pension plan, promises the participant a specified monthly benefit at retirement. Often, the benefit is based on factors such as your salary, your age, and the number of years you worked for the employer.

Defined Contribution Plan (DC Plan) - In a defined contribution plan, the employee and/or the employer contribute to the employee's individual account under the plan. The employee often decides how his or her account is invested. The amount in the account at distribution includes the contributions and investment gains or losses, minus any investment and administrative fees. The contributions and earnings are not taxed until distribution. The value of the account will change based on the value and performance of the investments.

ERISA - The Employee Retirement Income Security Act of 1974 is a Federal law that sets standards of protection for individuals in most voluntarily established, private-sector retirement plans. ERISA requires plans to provide participants with plan information, including important facts about plan features and funding; sets minimum standards for participation, vesting, benefit accrual, and funding; provides fiduciary responsibilities for those who manage and control plan assets; requires plans to establish a claims and appeals process for participants to get benefits from their plans; gives participants the right to sue for benefits and breaches of fiduciary duty.

Plan Administrator - The person who is identified in the plan document as having responsibility for running the plan. It could be the employer, a committee of employees, a company executive, or someone hired for that purpose.

Plan Document - A written instrument under which the plan is established and operated.

Plan Fiduciary - Anyone who exercises discretionary authority or discretionary control over management or administration of the plan, exercises any authority or control over management or disposition of plan assets, or gives investment advice for a fee or other compensation with respect to assets of the plan.

Plan Trustee - Someone who has the exclusive authority and discretion to manage and control the assets of the plan. The trustee can be subject to the direction of a named fiduciary and the named fiduciary can appoint one or more investment managers for the plan's assets.

Summary Plan Description (SPD) - A document provided by the plan administrator that includes a plain language description of important features of the plan, e.g., when employees begin to participate in the plan, how service and benefits are calculated, when benefits become vested, when payment is received and in what form, and how to file a claim for benefits. Participants must be informed of material changes either through a revised Summary Plan Description or in a separate document called a Summary of Material Modifications.

Vested Benefits - Those benefits that the individual has earned a right to receive and that cannot be forfeited.

Source: U.S. Department of Labor, Employee Benefits Security Administration, "What You Should Know about Your Retirement Plan"
http://www.dol.gov/ebsa/publications/wyskapr.html#glossary